The science in...

...a loaf of

BREAD

The science of changing materials and more...

Andrew Solway

W

FRANKLIN WATTS

LONDON • SYDNEY

First published in 2008
by Franklin Watts

Copyright © Franklin Watts 2008

Franklin Watts
338 Euston Road
London NW1 3BH

Franklin Watts Australia
Level 17/207 Kent Street
Sydney, NSW 2000

Planning and production by
Discovery Books Limited
Editor: Rebecca Hunter
Designer: Keith Williams
Illustrator: Stefan Chabluk
Photo researcher: Rachel Tisdale

Dewey number 530.4

ISBN 978 0 7496 8238 5

Printed in China

Franklin Watts is a division of Hachette
Children's Books, an Hachette Livre UK
company. www.hachettelivre.co.uk

Photo acknowledgements: istockphoto.com/Natalia
Klenova, front cover top; Getty Images/Neil Corder,
front cover bottom left; Discovery Picture Library,
front cover bottom right; istockphoto.com/Jason Alan,
p. 4; istockphoto.com/Dmitry Galanternik, p. 5;
istockphoto.com/Vera Bogaerts, p. 6; istockphoto.com/
Andrew Penner, p. 7; Corbis/Atlastide Phototravel, p. 9;
Corbis/David Turnley, p. 11 top; istockphoto.com/Vlado
Janzekovi, p11 bottom; Corbis/Visuals Unlimited, p. 12;
Corbis/Cultura, p. 14; Getty Images/Takako Chiba, p.
15; Getty Images/Neil Corder, p. 16; istockphoto.com, p.
17; istockphoto.com/Malgorzata Karpas, p. 18;
Corbis/Thomas A. Kelly, p. 19; istockphoto.com/Robyn
Mackenzie, p. 20; Shutterstock/H.D. Connelly, p. 21;
istockphoto.com/Dr. Heinz Linke, p. 23; Getty Images/
Dr. David M. Phillips, p. 25, istockphoto.com/Michael
Neale, p. 26; istockphoto.com/Peter Miller, p. 27;
istockphoto.com/Sergei Didyk, p. 28; istockphoto.com/
Alexander Hafemann, p. 29 top; istockphoto.com/
Paul Roux, p. 29 bottom.

Contents

Words that appear in **bold**
are in the glossary on page 30.

Smell that baking!

Mmm ... what's that smell? Someone is baking bread! Bread smells wonderful when it is cooking – and it tastes delicious when it is cooked. It has been a staple food in many parts of the world for thousands of years.

▲ *There is not just one kind of bread, there are many sorts. Above are some examples.*

Don't eat it raw!

Bread is basically just three **ingredients** – flour, yeast and water (with a little salt and oil). By themselves, the ingredients are not very tasty. Flour is ground-up grains of wheat or some other **cereal**. Have you tried eating it raw? Don't bother! It tastes horrible and could give you an upset stomach. Yeast is actually living – it is millions of tiny microbes. It doesn't taste nice raw either, and it would almost certainly upset your stomach. Water won't harm you, but it has no taste of its own.

Is it magic?

If you put flour, yeast and water together in the right way, and heat them up for a while, something happens. You don't get a nasty-tasting mush – you get delicious bread! What is going on here? Is it magic? You can learn all about bread, and the changes that happen as it is made, in this book. You can also find out about different kinds of bread, and how big bakeries produce thousands of loaves every day. You can even find out what happens to bread after you have eaten it. Best of all, there is an easy recipe for making bread that you can try out at home (make sure you get an adult to help).

Happy baking!

What is a staple food?

A **staple food** is a starchy food, something that people usually eat with most meals. In Europe, staple foods are things such as potatoes, or bread and pasta, which are made from wheat. In places such as India, Indonesia and southern China, rice is the main staple food. Other examples of staple foods are maize (corn), barley and yams.

▼ *Lentils, beans, rice and wheat (bottom right) are examples of staple foods.*

Why we eat bread

Have you eaten any bread today? Maybe you had some toast for breakfast, or a sandwich for lunch. Perhaps you had an Indian meal with naan bread or paratha. Or maybe you ate cheese on toast, or a pizza. Possibly for dessert you had summer pudding, bread and butter pudding or brown bread ice cream. All these foods contain bread.

Reasons to eat bread

Bread is a staple food, so most of us eat a lot of it. The main reason for this is that bread tastes good! However there are other reasons. For example, we can do lots of different things with bread. It is also cheap and widely available. Wheat grows well in large parts of North America, Europe and Asia.

Eating bread is good for us. Bread is mainly made up of starch, or **carbohydrate**. Carbohydrates are important types of food for the body. Starchy food is energy food, so bread can give us a large part of our daily energy needs.

▼ *In many parts of north Africa and the Middle East, people make flat bread using a large, curved, metal plate heated over a fire.*

Different nutrients

Some kinds of bread contain more **nutrients** than others. Carbohydrates are not the only nutrients our bodies need – we also need **protein**, fat and small amounts of **vitamins** and **minerals**. White bread is made from white wheat flour. When wheat is ground, the tougher parts, known as bran and wheatgerm, are removed to make white flour. This has plenty of carbohydrate, but little protein or fat.

Wholemeal bread is made from wholemeal flour. As its name suggests, wholemeal flour is made from the whole grain, with nothing removed. It contains more protein, vitamins and other nutrients than white flour. Multigrain breads have more than one kind of cereal in them, and breads such as Italian ciabatta bread have oil or fat in them. Each kind of bread has a different selection of nutrients.

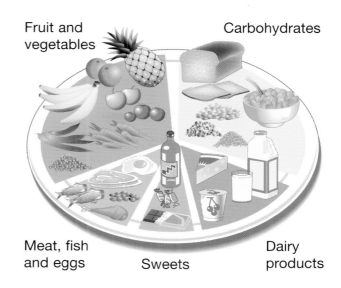

Fruit and vegetables

Carbohydrates

Meat, fish and eggs

Sweets

Dairy products

▲ *This food plate shows the types of food we should eat and in what proportions. Carbohydrates such as bread and pasta, and fruit and vegetables should make up the largest part of our diet. Foods such as meat, sweets and dairy products should be eaten in smaller quantities.*

Cereals

Wheat, rice, maize, barley, oats, rye, millet and sorghum are all kinds of cereals. Cereals are basically types of grass. The part that we eat is the grain (the seeds). Often the grains are ground into flour, but they can also be used in many other ways. Rice grains are most often cooked in water. Oats are often rolled to squash them (this makes oatmeal) before cooking. Corn and rice are sometimes heated until they burst open, to make popcorn or puffed rice. Breakfast cereals are made from – guess what?

▼ *Wheat being harvested in Canada. Canada is one of the world's largest wheat producers.*

An easy bread recipe

There is nothing better than a slice of home-made bread, warm and spread with butter. So how about making some? Making your own bread is the best way to understand the changes that happen in bread making. Here is a simple recipe. You will need an adult to help with the oven and maybe some of the other bits as well.

You will need:

500 g plain white flour
1 teaspoon salt
1 packet (7 g) dried fast-action yeast
2 tablespoons oil (olive oil is best)
300 ml warm water (hand-hot)

Also a greased baking tray, a jug, a mixing bowl and a wooden spoon.

What to do

First give your hands a good wash: you are going to 'knead' them!

1 Mix together the flour, salt and dried yeast in the bowl, using the spoon. Now make a well in the middle of the mixture.

2 Mix the oil and water, then pour the oily water into the well. Gradually mix the flour into the liquid, using the spoon at first and then your hands.

Take the dough out of the bowl and put it on a floured surface.

3 Now knead the dough. Use the heel of your hands to press the dough down and away from you. Then fold the dough over and press it down again.

4 Turn the dough a quarter turn and fold it over again. Keep pressing, folding and turning for 5 to 10 minutes. By this time the dough should be springy and elastic.

5 Put the dough in an oiled bowl, and cover it. Leave it in a warm place to rise for about an hour (it should double in size).

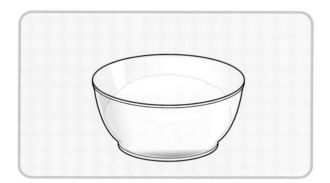

6 Punch down the dough, then gently shape it into a ball. Put it on the greased baking sheet. Cut a cross in the top of the dough with a knife, then leave it to rise in a warm place for another hour.

Here is where you need the adult.

7 Get them to put the loaf in a hot oven (220°C, 425°F, gas mark 7). Cook it for 25 to 30 minutes. When it is cooked it should be nicely browned, and sound hollow when you tap the bottom.

8 Leave your loaf to cool for a while on a wire rack. Then cut a slice, butter and eat. Delicious!

▼ *A baker's bread oven. The thick walls are made of brick, which keeps its heat. The baker puts bread in and takes it out with a long-handled wooden paddle.*

What is flour?

Now that you have seen how to bake bread at home, we will look more closely at the ingredients in bread. The most important one is the flour. It is the changes in the flour that turn bread from a soggy lump into a nice crusty loaf.

Inside a grain of wheat

Let's start by taking a closer look at a grain of wheat. Wheat grains are seeds. They have a hard, protective outer coat, to keep out insects. Inside the grain are two main parts. First there is the embryo itself. This is the part of the seed that can grow and become a plant. Then there is the endosperm. This is a store of food that the embryo can draw on when it starts to grow.

The different parts of the wheat grain are made of different substances. The embryo is rich in protein. The endosperm contains mostly starch, plus a small amount of protein. The outer coat is made of tough materials that we cannot **digest**.

Making flour

Flour is made by grinding up wheat grains. Most modern flour is made by grinding the grains between pairs of rollers. The flour is sieved in several ways to separate the fine, white endosperm from the bran (pieces of the hard seed coats) and wheatgerm (ground-up parts of the embryo). For white flour, only the fine flour is used. For wholemeal flour, the larger pieces of bran or wheatgerm are rolled again to grind them finer, then they are added back to the white flour.

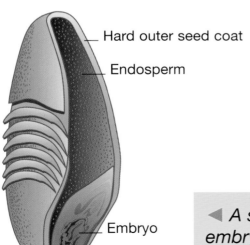

Hard outer seed coat

Endosperm

Embryo

◄ *A single wheat grain, cut open to show the embryo and endosperm inside.*

▲ *Milling flour in the traditional way, using a large millstone to crush the wheat grains. The result is stoneground flour.*

Bread-making flour

An important substance in flour is a protein called gluten (see pages 14-15). It is the substance that makes bread dough springy and elastic. It also traps the gas bubbles that make the bread rise. Bread-making flour or 'strong' flour, has more gluten than other kinds of flour.

Stoneground flour is made in a more traditional way, using millstones. These are two disc-shaped stones, one of which is fixed while the other turns. The grain is fed between the stones through a hole in the centre. The grains are crushed between the stones and ground into flour. Grooves in the moving stone allow the flour to escape at the outer edge.

▶ *This cereal crop is wheat. Once it is harvested, the grains are extracted and used to make flour.*

What is yeast?

For most kinds of bread, an important part of the process is letting the dough rise. To make this happen, you need yeast.

Useful microbe

Yeast is a microscopic living thing. It is a type of **fungus**, a relative of mushrooms and toadstools. Each yeast microbe is a single living cell, shaped like a fat rugby ball.

Yeasts like some of the same foods as us, particularly starch or sugars. When they have plenty of food (such as the starch in bread flour), they reproduce rapidly. This process is called **budding**. As they grow, they

▼ *A magnified image of yeast cells. The cell in the centre is budding.*

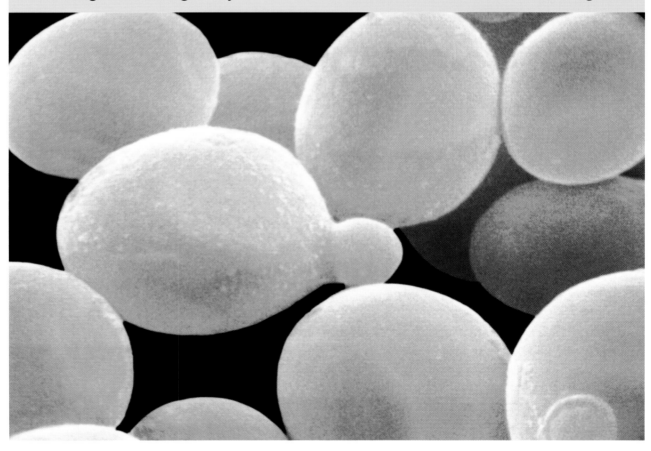

Yeasty gas

Try this experiment to show that growing yeast produces gas.

You will need:
- 1 packet of dried, rapid-action yeast
- 1 cup of hand-hot water
- 2 tablespoons of sugar
- a jug and spoon
- a jar or bottle that holds about 0.5 litres
- a small plastic bag
- an elastic band

What to do:

1 Mix the yeast, water and sugar well in the jug. After a short time, you should see the mixture start to bubble.

2 Pour the mixture into the jar or bottle.

3 Fasten the plastic bag over the mouth of the jar or bottle, using the elastic band. Make sure the elastic is tight, so that there is no leakage.

4 After a short time, the plastic bag should start to fill up with gas produced by the yeast mixture.

produce alcohol and the gas **carbon dioxide** as waste products. This process is called **fermentation**. The carbon dioxide produced gets trapped in tiny pockets inside the dough, and makes it rise.

Yeasts add to the flavour of the bread as well as making it rise. Yeasts are full of special proteins called **enzymes**. These enzymes can break down the starch in flour into other, simpler substances such as weak acids (like the acids in apple juice and lemon juice). These simple chemicals give the baked bread a much nicer flavour than the raw flour.

Yeasts are everywhere!

Baker's yeast is a particular kind of yeast. It is commonly found on the skins of grapes and plums, where it grows naturally. However, there are yeasts around us all the time – there are probably some yeast cells on your skin right now.

Using yeast to make bread rise probably happened accidentally in the first place. Thousands of years ago, someone perhaps made dough for flat bread, then left it for some time before cooking it. Yeast that had got into the dough naturally could have made the dough rise.

From flour to dough

We know a bit more about the main ingredients in our bread now. So let's look at what happens when we start to make the bread.

Starting the yeast

In the easy bread recipe on pages 8-9, we mixed in the yeast with the flour and salt, then added the liquid. However, some recipes get you to check that the yeast is working properly by proving it. The yeast is mixed with some warm water and a tablespoon or so of sugar, or some flour. The mixture is then left for a time. If the yeast is working properly, the mixture froths up as carbon dioxide is formed.

Adding water

Adding water to the flour and yeast is what starts the whole bread-making process off. Dried yeast can be stored in a cool, dark place without anything happening to it at all. Similarly, flour can be stored for months without changing. However, once water is added to them both, changes start to happen very quickly.

We have seen already how adding warm water to yeast starts the yeast microbes growing and dividing. But what happens to the flour? The water makes two important things happen. First, the starch in the flour soaks up water and swells. Second, two kinds of protein in the flour begin to connect up with each other to form another kind of protein – gluten.

Kneading the dough

It is possible to make bread without kneading the dough. However, kneading helps in two ways. First, it mixes the ingredients in the bread thoroughly, which makes the dough consistent (with no odd lumps or holes). Second, it speeds up the process of gluten formation, helping to form the gluten into elastic sheets.

When the dough has been well-kneaded, it is strong and can be formed easily into different shapes. You could try this yourself next time you make bread. For instance, you could split your dough into three equal pieces, and roll them out into long sausages. Then plait the three sausages together to make a loaf known as a plait.

◀ *The gluten in flour helps to make dough stretchy and flexible. Without gluten, this man would not be able to stretch pizza dough into a thin pancake.*

▲ *In Japan and China, gluten is used in cooking. It can be deep-fried or steamed, or used to make some kinds of wagashi (Japanese sweets), as shown here.*

Leaving bread to rise

We saw on pages 12-13 what makes bread rise –
it is carbon dioxide produced by the yeast in the dough.
Letting the dough rise makes the bread light and easier
to eat. The way that bread rises depends on the
conditions that the bread is made in.

Keeping conditions right

It is important to keep the yeast cells growing strongly while bread is being made. This is why we add hand-hot water to the dough, and why we put it in a warm place to rise. When yeast cells are warm, they grow more quickly. This means they produce more carbon dioxide, and the bread rises faster. However, the water must not be too hot. If we used boiling water to make the dough, it would kill the yeast and the bread would not rise at all.

Yeast will still grow, and bread will still rise, at a lower temperature. For instance, if you leave dough in the fridge overnight, it will rise as much as it does in an hour in a warm place. However, if the dough is kept warm for a time and then becomes cold, the dough will go wrong. The gas that is already trapped in the bread will shrink, and the dough will sink.

▲ *When dough rises it fills with bubbles of carbon dioxide gas. This makes it expand.*

Bread without yeast

Have you heard of unleavened bread? It is flat bread, made without yeast. Naan bread and pitta bread are both types of unleavened bread. There are many other kinds of flat bread made in different parts of the world.

Some kinds of bread are made using other methods to make them rise. You can find out about them on pages 20-21.

▲ *In a hot air balloon, a gas burner heats the air inside the balloon. The hot air expands and makes the balloon rise. In the same way, when yeast is warmed it produces carbon dioxide which causes the bread dough to rise.*

Changing gases

Like the yeast itself, the carbon dioxide gas produced when bread rises is affected by temperature. This is because the amount of space a certain amount of gas takes up depends on its temperature. As the gas gets warmer, it expands and takes up more space. As it cools down it contracts (shrinks) and takes up less space. You can see this for yourself by trying this experiment: Blow up a balloon, and measure around it with a tape measure or a piece of string. Put it in the fridge for an hour or so, then take it out of the fridge and measure it again. You will find that the balloon is quite a lot smaller than when it went in.

Changes during cooking

Now that the bread has been kneaded and risen, it is ready to go in the oven. What changes happen when it is baked?

The effects of heat

When you put the bread in the oven, lots of things start to happen. First, as the dough gets hotter, the gases trapped inside the bread get hotter too. This makes them expand, and the bread grows even more. At first the yeast in the bread grows more quickly because of the heat. But then it gets hotter, it becomes too hot for the yeast cells, and they die. Now no more carbon dioxide is produced.

The heat also dries out the bread, because some of the water in the dough evaporates (turns to gas). Some other substances in the bread, such as alcohol, evaporate too, which changes the way the bread tastes.

Other changes, called browning reactions, affect the outside of the bread, which becomes harder and goes brown. Once the top of the bread has browned and the bottom sounds hollow, the bread is ready.

◄ The outside of a crusty loaf of bread is tough, but once you cut through the crust the inside is soft and chewy.

▲ *Bagels, cooked to perfection, in a New York bakery.*

Why so hot?

Bread is always cooked at a high temperature – almost the highest setting on the oven. This is to cook the outside of the bread quickly, to harden it into a crust, without making the inside of the bread hard, too. Most people like bread best when it has a nice, crunchy outer crust and a soft, springy inside. If the bread were cooked at a lower temperature, it would take longer to heat through. The crust would be too thick and the whole loaf would become tough and hard.

Bread ovens

The ovens that professional bakers use are specially designed to give the bread a nice crust. There are two main differences from the oven you may have at home. First, the oven has thick walls that retain heat well. The oven takes a long time to heat up, but once it is hot it stays hot for a long time. This means that the oven does not cool down much when it is opened to put bread in.

The second difference is that most bread ovens are steam ovens. Steam is injected into the oven while the bread cooks. Having steam in the oven is a very good way of developing a good crust on the bread.

Other types of bread

Sourdough and soda bread are two kinds of bread that do not use normal baker's yeast. Sourdough bread uses a mixture of microbes, while soda bread uses no microbes at all.

Sourdough

Sourdough is a traditional type of bread that involves taking advantage of the yeasts and other microbes that are naturally found in flour. The bread is made to rise using a starter dough. This is made by mixing flour with water and leaving it for several days, to allow microbes to grow in the mixture. Later, the dough is refreshed by adding more flour and water. After refreshing it several times, the starter dough reaches a stage where it has a stable balance of microbes in it. Some of the microbes are yeasts, but wild yeasts rather than baker's yeast. The other microbes in the starter dough are certain kinds of bacteria. The yeasts produce carbon dioxide, while the bacteria produce a weak acid, which gives sourdough bread its special taste.

◀ *Sourdough bread is nice with ham and cheese!*

Soda bread

Soda bread is a kind of bread made especially in Ireland, that can be prepared quickly. Instead of using yeast, soda bread uses a combination of baking soda (sodium bicarbonate) and buttermilk to make the bread rise. The soda and buttermilk are mixed with flour, water and salt to make the dough. The buttermilk is acid, and when it combines with the soda, a chemical reaction happens. One of the products of this reaction is – guess what – carbon dioxide! This makes the soda bread rise.

Irish bread

Soda bread is most commonly made in Ireland (although American cornbread is also made with soda and buttermilk). It was first made there in about 1840, when baking soda was introduced into the country. The climate in Ireland makes it hard to grow the kind of wheat that works best for making traditional bread. Bread made using soda and buttermilk worked better with the kind of flour that could be produced in Ireland.

► *Soda bread is a type of bread that uses baking soda and buttermilk instead of yeast. Other ingredients can be added such as raisins and nuts.*

Buttermilk

Buttermilk is cow's milk that has been treated to give it a sour taste. Traditional buttermilk was the liquid left over after churning cream to make butter. However, buttermilk is often made today by adding special bacteria to the milk. The bacteria produce acid, which gives the buttermilk a sour taste.

A commercial bakery

Bread made in a commercial bakery is made in large amounts. The dough is made about a tonne at a time, and thousands of loaves are made every day. So how is it done?

Making the dough

In the first stage, the yeast, water and about three-quarters of the flour are mixed together to make a sponge. This then sits in a warm room for a few hours, until it stops rising and begins to fall.

▼ *The stages of making bread in a commercial bakery.*

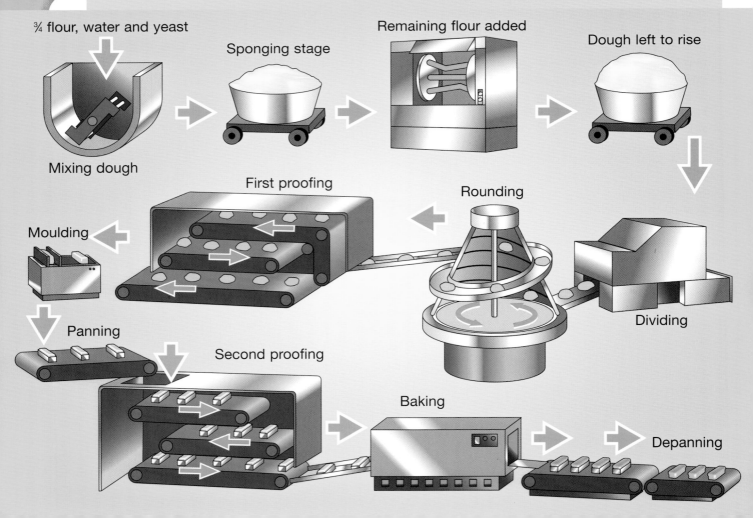

¾ flour, water and yeast

Sponging stage

Remaining flour added

Dough left to rise

Mixing dough

First proofing

Rounding

Moulding

Dividing

Panning

Second proofing

Baking

Depanning

▶ *Dough is mixed on a large scale in this commercial bakery.*

Now the rest of the flour is mixed in to make the dough. It goes back to the warm room to rise again.

Shaping

The finished dough is ready for cutting and shaping. It goes through a dividing machine that cuts the dough into loaf-sized pieces, then another that rounds the pieces up. By this time the dough has lost some of its air and elasticity. It is left to rest for a few minutes (first proofing stage) before it is moulded into shapes and put into pans (bread tins). The dough is then left to rise for another 20 minutes (second proofing) before baking.

Baking

Commercial bread ovens are often designed to have a continuous line of loaves going through them. Tunnel ovens have a conveyor belt that takes the loaves through a long, hot tunnel. The bread is baked when it comes out the other end. Chamber ovens also have a conveyor belt, but it runs in a spiral through a large heated chamber. As they come out of the oven, the loaves are tipped or sucked out of their pans. The loaves are then cooled on racks before being packed and sent off to the shops.

Bread additives

Bread that is made commercially has to keep longer than home-made bread. The dough also has to be consistent (come out right every time). A baker can't afford to throw away a tonne of dough because it has not risen properly!

To help the bread keep longer and come out well every time, bakers add small amounts of chemicals to the bread. Substances called emulsifiers, for instance, stop the bread from going stale quickly. Other additives, called dough conditioners, are used to help make sure that the dough rises well and is strong.

All the additives used in bread are harmless. However, some people feel that they are unnecessary, and will only eat bread without additives.

Digesting bread

So now we get to the best part of baking – eating the bread! When we eat a slice of bread and honey, or munch a cheese sandwich, we enjoy the taste, chew and then swallow. After that, the bread has gone – we don't think about it any more. But in fact it still has a long journey ahead, through our digestive system.

Why do we need to digest bread?

We have seen that bread is made mainly of carbohydrates, proteins and a small amount of fat. Our bodies cannot use these complex substances directly. They need to be broken down into simpler nutrients that can be absorbed into the blood. The nutrients can then be used in different parts of the body.

Stages of digestion

Digestion of bread begins in the mouth. The saliva (spit) begins to break down the starch in the bread into sugars. Like yeasts, the digestive system uses enzymes to help break down the carbohydrates and other substances in bread.

After it has been chewed and swallowed, it passes down the oesophagus to the stomach. Here it is mixed with acid and other

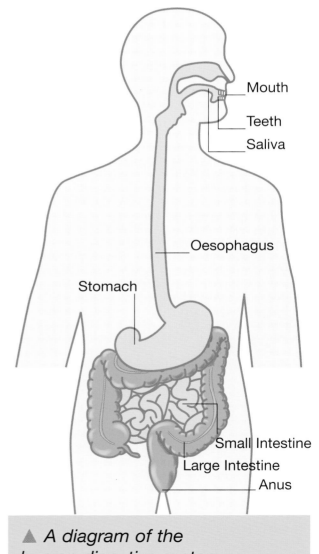

Mouth
Teeth
Saliva
Oesophagus
Stomach
Small Intestine
Large Intestine
Anus

▲ *A diagram of the human digestive system.*

liquids. The stomach is a large bag where food can be stored and mixed. The proteins in the bread start to break down here.

From the stomach, the mixed food goes into a long tube called the small intestine. In the first part of the small intestine, the carbohydrates, proteins and fats are completely broken down into useful nutrients. In the second part of the small intestine, these nutrients are absorbed by the **villi** into the blood.

The last part of the digestion process happens in the large intestine. This is another tube, wider than the small

Fibre

Foods such as wholemeal bread and brown rice are rich in fibre. Fibre is a kind of carbohydrate. A lot of it is material that we cannot digest (break down into nutrients). This kind of fibre helps the digestive system to work properly. Other kinds of fibre help our bodies to get a steady supply of energy and protect us against heart disease.

intestine. The bran from the bread, and other parts that we cannot digest, go into this section. Water is absorbed from the waste, then it leaves the body through the anus when you go to the toilet.

▼ *This microscope photograph shows the tiny, finger-like villi that cover the inside of the small intestine.*

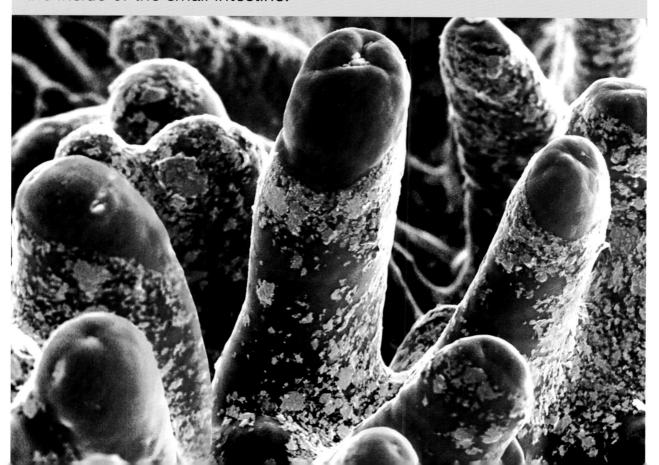

Reversible changes

In science there are two types of changes, reversible and irreversible. Reversible changes can be reversed and irreversible changes cannot. Bread making involves both of these changes. First, we will look at the reversible changes.

Sieving

When you put together the dry ingredients in bread, you get a mixture. The ingredients have been combined, but you can separate them again. The mixing is a physical change, and it is reversible.

There are several ways to separate mixtures. The easiest way to separate solids is to sieve them.

The flour, salt and yeast in bread can be separated in this way. The grains of flour will pass through a fine sieve, but the yeast and salt will not. A sieve with slightly larger holes will separate the yeast from the salt.

Filtering

Filtering is a way of separating solids from liquids. It is like sieving, but the solid particles are often smaller, so the sieve has to be finer. When you make coffee, you mix together ground coffee beans and hot water. Some of the coffee **dissolves** in the water and gives it flavour, but you need to get rid of the bits of ground coffee that don't dissolve. You can do this by pouring it through a filter. The liquid coffee passes through the paper filter, but the solid coffee grounds are held back.

◀ *Some solids can be separated by sieving them.*

26

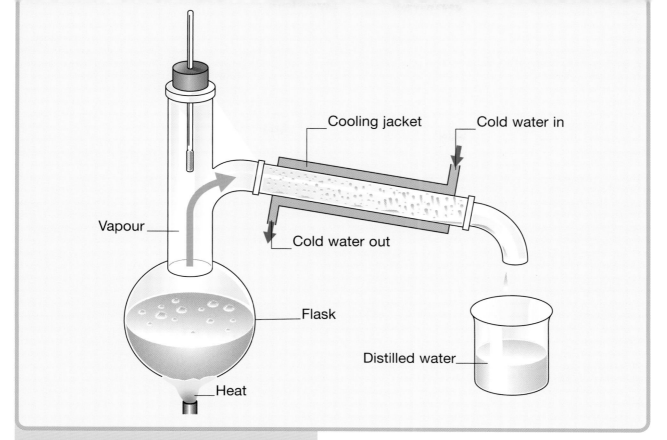

Cooling jacket

Cold water in

Vapour

Cold water out

Flask

Distilled water

Heat

▲ *This distillation apparatus can be used to separate a solution (mixture) of salt and water.*

Distillation

When you dissolve a solid in a liquid, you create a solution. It would seem that this change is irreversible as you can no longer see the solid. But even this mixture can be separated. If you make a salt solution by mixing salt and water, it is possible to separate the salt and water by the process of distillation. This diagram above shows you how. The salt solution is heated until it boils. The water evaporates and is then cooled so it condenses. Pure water can be collected and solid salt crystals will eventually be left in the bottom of the flask.

Fractional distillation

Distillation is useful for other things besides getting salt out of a solution. A special kind of distillation, known as fractional distillation, is used to get petrol and other useful substances from **crude oil**. This is a distillation tower at an oil refinery in Cardiff.

Irreversible changes

Many of the changes in bread making are irreversible. A chemical change takes place. This means that the ingredients react together and change each other. Chemical changes are much harder to reverse than physical ones. The chemical changes that happen in bread-making are irreversible. The loaf of bread you take out of the oven cannot be turned back into flour, water and yeast.

Baking reactions

When you bake bread, several chemical reactions take place at the same time. First, two proteins in the flour combine chemically to form gluten. There is no gluten in the flour initially, but when the flour is mixed with water and kneaded, gluten is formed.

The yeast in the bread also sets off some chemical reactions. It converts the sugars (starch) in the bread into carbon dioxide gas and other by-products. The gas is what causes the bread to rise and gives it a spongy texture. When the dough is baked, the yeast is killed and these chemical reactions stop.

Other chemical changes

Another chemical reaction that you are probably familiar with is burning or **combustion**. Many different things burn, but they all involve the same kind of chemical reaction. Most things that burn, such as paper, wood, coal, oil and petrol, contain a lot of carbon. When they burn, the carbon in them combines with oxygen from the air.

◄ *Heat sets off chemical reactions in food which is being cooked.*

Reactions around us

There are many other chemical reactions going on around us. Some are very simple. When a piece of metal goes rusty, for instance, it is caused by a single chemical reaction between iron and oxygen in the air. Oxygen reacts with iron to form iron oxide (rust). This chemical reaction is usually very slow. It can take weeks or months for a piece of iron to rust.

▲ *Rusting is a slower chemical reaction than burning. Over, days, months and years, iron gradually reacts with air to form iron oxide (rust).*

▼ *If you leave bread in the toaster too long, you might end up getting combustion instead of cooking.*

Glossary

budding when an organism is growing and separating to form a new individual, such as in the reproduction of yeast cells

carbohydrate a kind of nutrient in food that gives you energy. Sugars and starch are carbohydrates

carbon dioxide a gas in the air

cereal a grass-like plant such as rice, wheat or oats, the seeds of which are used as food

combustion the process of burning

crude oil or petroleum is a substance found in the ground that is used to make fuels, plastics, motor oil, paints, polishes and many other products

digest to break down food chemically into simple nutrients that the body can absorb and use

dissolves when a solid mixes completely with water so that it is no longer visible, it has dissolved

enzymes proteins that control the chemical reactions in living things

fermentation the chemical breakdown of a substance using yeasts or other micro-organisms

fungi a large group of plant-like living things that includes mushrooms, moulds and yeasts

ingredients the different things that are mixed together to make bread or some other food

minerals simple chemicals, such as calcium and iron, that are needed in small amounts in the diet

nutrients simple substances that the body needs to survive and grow

proteins complex chemicals that carry out several important jobs in living things

staple food a cheap, starchy food such as bread, rice or potatoes that is a major part of the diet

villi the small, finger-like projections that line the small intestine

vitamins substances found in food that we need to eat in small amounts to be healthy

Further information

Websites

Science of Bread: Kitchen Lab
www.exploratorium.edu/cooking/
bread/kitchenlab.html

Learn about the science of baking and try some experiments at this website from the Exploratorium Museum, San Francisco.

The Story Behind a Loaf of Bread
www.botham.co.uk/bread/

The history of bread, commercial baking, wheat, bread ovens and bread-making superstitions are all on this excellent website.

The Easiest Way to Make the Best Bread
www.aboutscotland.com/cuisine/
index.html

Another simple bread recipe, with lots of tips about how to make your loaves delicious every time.

The History of Bread Yeast
www.bbc.co.uk/dna/h2g2/A2791820

Learn more about what bread is, how yeast was used in ancient Egypt and why it was banned by Parisian doctors in the 17th century.

Note to parents and teachers: Every effort has been made by the publishers to ensure that these websites are suitable for children, that they are of the highest educational value, and that they contain no inappropriate or offensive material. However, because of the nature of the Internet, it is impossible to guarantee that the contents of these sites will not be altered. We strongly advise that Internet access is supervised by a responsible adult.

Index